This
Pet Journal
belongs to

_____

_____

Pet Profile

Pet Name:	Color:
Breed:	Birthday:
Sex:	Breed:

Microchip info.	Medical condition

Personality traits	Habits

Pet Photo

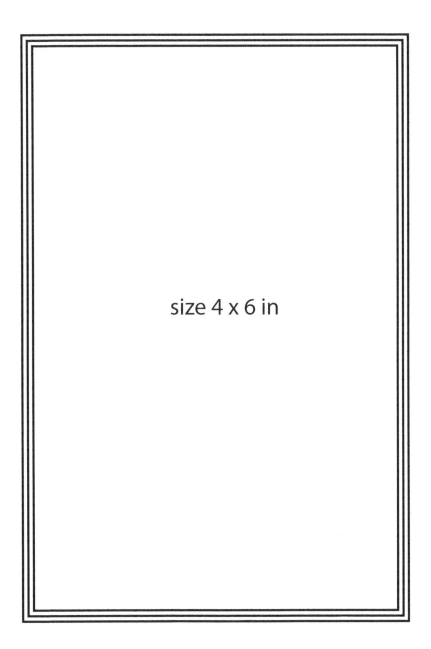

size 4 x 6 in

Emergency contacts

Name	Phone

Vet Visits

Date	Purpose	Clinic name

Vaccinations

Date	Weight	Against

Vaccinations

Veterinarian	Clinic name	Comments

Daily Log

Wake up at:

Activity level:

Food and treats

Time	Food and Amount

Water Intake

Time	Amount

Bathroom/Pee, Poo	Medications/ Time, Dosage

Daily Log

Wake up at:

Activity level:

Food and treats

Time	Food and Amount

Water Intake

Time	Amount

Bathroom/Pee, Poo	Medications/ Time, Dosage

Daily Log

Wake up at:

Activity level:

Food and treats

Time	Food and Amount

Water Intake

Time	Amount

Bathroom/Pee, Poo	Medications/ Time, Dosage

Daily Log

Wake up at:

Activity level:

Food and treats

Time	Food and Amount

Water Intake

Time	Amount

Bathroom/Pee, Poo	Medications/ Time, Dosage

Daily Log

Wake up at:

Activity level:

Food and treats

Time	Food and Amount

Water Intake

Time	Amount

Bathroom/Pee, Poo	Medications/ Time, Dosage

Daily Log

Wake up at:

Activity level:

Food and treats

Time	Food and Amount

Water Intake

Time	Amount

Bathroom/Pee, Poo	Medications/ Time, Dosage

Daily Log

Wake up at:

Activity level:

Food and treats

Time	Food and Amount

Water Intake

Time	Amount

Bathroom/Pee, Poo	Medications/ Time, Dosage

Daily Log

Wake up at:

Activity level:

Food and treats

Time	Food and Amount

Water Intake

Time	Amount

Bathroom/Pee, Poo	Medications/ Time, Dosage

Daily Log

Wake up at:

Activity level:

Food and treats

Time	Food and Amount

Water Intake

Time	Amount

Bathroom/Pee, Poo	Medications/ Time, Dosage

Daily Log

Wake up at:

Activity level:

Food and treats

Time	Food and Amount

Water Intake

Time	Amount

Bathroom/Pee, Poo	Medications/ Time, Dosage

Daily Log

Wake up at:

Activity level:

Food and treats

Time	Food and Amount

Water Intake

Time	Amount

Bathroom/Pee, Poo	Medications/ Time, Dosage

Daily Log

Wake up at:

Activity level:

Food and treats

Time	Food and Amount

Water Intake

Time	Amount

Bathroom/Pee, Poo	Medications/ Time, Dosage

Daily Log

Wake up at:

Activity level:

Food and treats

Time	Food and Amount

Water Intake

Time	Amount

Bathroom/Pee, Poo	Medications/ Time, Dosage

Daily Log

Wake up at:

Activity level:

Food and treats

Time	Food and Amount

Water Intake

Time	Amount

Bathroom/Pee, Poo	Medications/ Time, Dosage

Daily Log

Wake up at:

Activity level:

Food and treats

Time	Food and Amount

Water Intake

Time	Amount

Bathroom/Pee, Poo	Medications/ Time, Dosage

Daily Log

Wake up at:

Activity level:

Food and treats

Time	Food and Amount

Water Intake

Time	Amount

Bathroom/Pee, Poo	Medications/ Time, Dosage

Daily Log

Wake up at:

Activity level:

Food and treats

Time	Food and Amount

Water Intake

Time	Amount

Bathroom/Pee, Poo	Medications/ Time, Dosage

Daily Log

Wake up at:

Activity level:

Food and treats

Time	Food and Amount

Water Intake

Time	Amount

Bathroom/Pee, Poo	Medications/ Time, Dosage

Daily Log

Wake up at:

Activity level:

Food and treats

Time	Food and Amount

Water Intake

Time	Amount

Bathroom/Pee, Poo	Medications/ Time, Dosage

Daily Log

Wake up at:

Activity level:

Food and treats

Time	Food and Amount

Water Intake

Time	Amount

Bathroom/Pee, Poo	Medications/ Time, Dosage

Daily Log

Wake up at:

Activity level:

Food and treats

Time	Food and Amount

Water Intake

Time	Amount

Bathroom/Pee, Poo	Medications/ Time, Dosage

Daily Log

Wake up at:

Activity level:

Food and treats

Time	Food and Amount

Water Intake

Time	Amount

Bathroom/Pee, Poo	Medications/ Time, Dosage

Daily Log

Wake up at:

Activity level:

Food and treats

Time	Food and Amount

Water Intake

Time	Amount

Bathroom/Pee, Poo	Medications/ Time, Dosage

Daily Log

Wake up at:

Activity level:

Food and treats

Time	Food and Amount

Water Intake

Time	Amount

Bathroom/Pee, Poo	Medications/ Time, Dosage

Daily Log

Wake up at:

Activity level:

Food and treats

Time	Food and Amount

Water Intake

Time	Amount

Bathroom/Pee, Poo	Medications/ Time, Dosage

Daily Log

Wake up at:

Activity level:

Food and treats

Time	Food and Amount

Water Intake

Time	Amount

Bathroom/Pee, Poo	Medications/ Time, Dosage

Daily Log

Wake up at:

Activity level:

Food and treats

Time	Food and Amount

Water Intake

Time	Amount

Bathroom/Pee, Poo	Medications/ Time, Dosage

Daily Log

Wake up at:

Activity level:

Food and treats

Time	Food and Amount

Water Intake

Time	Amount

Bathroom/Pee, Poo	Medications/ Time, Dosage

Daily Log

Wake up at:

Activity level:

Food and treats

Time	Food and Amount

Water Intake

Time	Amount

Bathroom/Pee, Poo	Medications/ Time, Dosage

Daily Log

Wake up at:

Activity level:

Food and treats

Time	Food and Amount

Water Intake

Time	Amount

Bathroom/Pee, Poo	Medications/ Time, Dosage

Daily Log

Wake up at:

Activity level:

Food and treats

Time	Food and Amount

Water Intake

Time	Amount

Bathroom/Pee, Poo	Medications/ Time, Dosage

Daily Log

Wake up at:

Activity level:

Food and treats

Time	Food and Amount

Water Intake

Time	Amount

Bathroom/Pee, Poo	Medications/ Time, Dosage

Daily Log

Wake up at:

Activity level:

Food and treats

Time	Food and Amount

Water Intake

Time	Amount

Bathroom/Pee, Poo	Medications/ Time, Dosage

Daily Log

Wake up at:

Activity level:

Food and treats

Time	Food and Amount

Water Intake

Time	Amount

Bathroom/Pee, Poo	Medications/ Time, Dosage

Daily Log

Wake up at:

Activity level:

Food and treats

Time	Food and Amount

Water Intake

Time	Amount

Bathroom/Pee, Poo	Medications/ Time, Dosage

Daily Log

Wake up at:

Activity level:

Food and treats

Time	Food and Amount

Water Intake

Time	Amount

Bathroom/Pee, Poo	Medications/ Time, Dosage

Daily Log

Wake up at:

Activity level:

Food and treats

Time	Food and Amount

Water Intake

Time	Amount

Bathroom/Pee, Poo	Medications/ Time, Dosage

Daily Log

Wake up at:

Activity level:

Food and treats

Time	Food and Amount

Water Intake

Time	Amount

Bathroom/Pee, Poo	Medications/ Time, Dosage

Daily Log

Wake up at:

Activity level:

Food and treats

Time	Food and Amount

Water Intake

Time	Amount

Bathroom/Pee, Poo	Medications/ Time, Dosage

Daily Log

Wake up at:

Activity level:

Food and treats

Time	Food and Amount

Water Intake

Time	Amount

Bathroom/Pee, Poo	Medications/ Time, Dosage

Daily Log

Wake up at:

Activity level:

Food and treats

Time	Food and Amount

Water Intake

Time	Amount

Bathroom/Pee, Poo	Medications/ Time, Dosage

Daily Log

Wake up at:

Activity level:

Food and treats

Time	Food and Amount

Water Intake

Time	Amount

Bathroom/Pee, Poo	Medications/ Time, Dosage

Daily Log

Wake up at:

Activity level:

Food and treats

Time	Food and Amount

Water Intake

Time	Amount

Bathroom/Pee, Poo	Medications/ Time, Dosage

Daily Log

Wake up at:

Activity level:

Food and treats

Time	Food and Amount

Water Intake

Time	Amount

Bathroom/Pee, Poo	Medications/ Time, Dosage

Daily Log

Wake up at:

Activity level:

Food and treats

Time	Food and Amount

Water Intake

Time	Amount

Bathroom/Pee, Poo	Medications/ Time, Dosage

Daily Log

Wake up at:

Activity level:

Food and treats

Time	Food and Amount

Water Intake

Time	Amount

Bathroom/Pee, Poo	Medications/ Time, Dosage

Daily Log

Wake up at:

Activity level:

Food and treats

Time	Food and Amount

Water Intake

Time	Amount

Bathroom/Pee, Poo	Medications/ Time, Dosage

Daily Log

Wake up at:

Activity level:

Food and treats

Time	Food and Amount

Water Intake

Time	Amount

Bathroom/Pee, Poo	Medications/ Time, Dosage

Daily Log

Wake up at:

Activity level:

Food and treats

Time	Food and Amount

Water Intake

Time	Amount

Bathroom/Pee, Poo	Medications/ Time, Dosage

Daily Log

Wake up at:

Activity level:

Food and treats

Time	Food and Amount

Water Intake

Time	Amount

Bathroom/Pee, Poo	Medications/ Time, Dosage

Daily Log

Wake up at:

Activity level:

Food and treats

Time	Food and Amount

Water Intake

Time	Amount

Bathroom/Pee, Poo	Medications/ Time, Dosage

Daily Log

Wake up at:

Activity level:

Food and treats

Time	Food and Amount

Water Intake

Time	Amount

Bathroom/Pee, Poo	Medications/ Time, Dosage

Daily Log

Wake up at:

Activity level:

Food and treats

Time	Food and Amount

Water Intake

Time	Amount

Bathroom/Pee, Poo	Medications/ Time, Dosage

Daily Log

Wake up at:

Activity level:

Food and treats

Time	Food and Amount

Water Intake

Time	Amount

Bathroom/Pee, Poo	Medications/ Time, Dosage

Daily Log

Wake up at:

Activity level:

Food and treats

Time	Food and Amount

Water Intake

Time	Amount

Bathroom/Pee, Poo	Medications/ Time, Dosage

Daily Log

Wake up at:

Activity level:

Food and treats

Time	Food and Amount

Water Intake

Time	Amount

Bathroom/Pee, Poo	Medications/ Time, Dosage

Daily Log

Wake up at:

Activity level:

Food and treats

Time	Food and Amount

Water Intake

Time	Amount

Bathroom/Pee, Poo	Medications/ Time, Dosage

Daily Log

Wake up at:

Activity level:

Food and treats

Time	Food and Amount

Water Intake

Time	Amount

Bathroom/Pee, Poo	Medications/ Time, Dosage

Daily Log

Wake up at:

Activity level:

Food and treats

Time	Food and Amount

Water Intake

Time	Amount

Bathroom/Pee, Poo	Medications/ Time, Dosage

Daily Log

Wake up at:

Activity level:

Food and treats

Time	Food and Amount

Water Intake

Time	Amount

Bathroom/Pee, Poo	Medications/ Time, Dosage

Daily Log

Wake up at:

Activity level:

Food and treats

Time	Food and Amount

Water Intake

Time	Amount

Bathroom/Pee, Poo	Medications/ Time, Dosage

Daily Log

Wake up at:

Activity level:

Food and treats

Time	Food and Amount

Water Intake

Time	Amount

Bathroom/Pee, Poo	Medications/ Time, Dosage

Daily Log

Wake up at:

Activity level:

Food and treats

Time	Food and Amount

Water Intake

Time	Amount

Bathroom/Pee, Poo	Medications/ Time, Dosage

Daily Log

Wake up at:

Activity level:

Food and treats

Time	Food and Amount

Water Intake

Time	Amount

Bathroom/Pee, Poo	Medications/ Time, Dosage

Daily Log

Wake up at:

Activity level:

Food and treats

Time	Food and Amount

Water Intake

Time	Amount

Bathroom/Pee, Poo	Medications/ Time, Dosage

Daily Log

Wake up at:

Activity level:

Food and treats

Time	Food and Amount

Water Intake

Time	Amount

Bathroom/Pee, Poo	Medications/ Time, Dosage

Daily Log

Wake up at:

Activity level:

Food and treats

Time	Food and Amount

Water Intake

Time	Amount

Bathroom/Pee, Poo	Medications/ Time, Dosage

Daily Log

Wake up at:

Activity level:

Food and treats

Time	Food and Amount

Water Intake

Time	Amount

Bathroom/Pee, Poo	Medications/ Time, Dosage

Daily Log

Wake up at:

Activity level:

Food and treats

Time	Food and Amount

Water Intake

Time	Amount

Bathroom/Pee, Poo	Medications/ Time, Dosage

Daily Log

Wake up at:

Activity level:

Food and treats

Time	Food and Amount

Water Intake

Time	Amount

Bathroom/Pee, Poo	Medications/ Time, Dosage

Daily Log

Wake up at:

Activity level:

Food and treats

Time	Food and Amount

Water Intake

Time	Amount

Bathroom/Pee, Poo	Medications/ Time, Dosage

Daily Log

Wake up at:

Activity level:

Food and treats

Time	Food and Amount

Water Intake

Time	Amount

Bathroom/Pee, Poo	Medications/ Time, Dosage

Daily Log

Wake up at:

Activity level:

Food and treats

Time	Food and Amount

Water Intake

Time	Amount

Bathroom/Pee, Poo	Medications/ Time, Dosage

Daily Log

Wake up at:

Activity level:

Food and treats

Time	Food and Amount

Water Intake

Time	Amount

Bathroom/Pee, Poo	Medications/ Time, Dosage

Daily Log

Wake up at:

Activity level:

Food and treats

Time	Food and Amount

Water Intake

Time	Amount

Bathroom/Pee, Poo	Medications/ Time, Dosage

Daily Log

Wake up at:

Activity level:

Food and treats

Time	Food and Amount

Water Intake

Time	Amount

Bathroom/Pee, Poo	Medications/ Time, Dosage

Daily Log

Wake up at:

Activity level:

Food and treats

Time	Food and Amount

Water Intake

Time	Amount

Bathroom/Pee, Poo	Medications/ Time, Dosage

Daily Log

Wake up at:

Activity level:

Food and treats

Time	Food and Amount

Water Intake

Time	Amount

Bathroom/Pee, Poo	Medications/ Time, Dosage

Daily Log

Wake up at:

Activity level:

Food and treats

Time	Food and Amount

Water Intake

Time	Amount

Bathroom/Pee, Poo	Medications/ Time, Dosage

Daily Log

Wake up at:

Activity level:

Food and treats

Time	Food and Amount

Water Intake

Time	Amount

Bathroom/Pee, Poo	Medications/ Time, Dosage

Daily Log

Wake up at:

Activity level:

Food and treats

Time	Food and Amount

Water Intake

Time	Amount

Bathroom/Pee, Poo	Medications/ Time, Dosage

Daily Log

Wake up at:

Activity level:

Food and treats

Time	Food and Amount

Water Intake

Time	Amount

Bathroom/Pee, Poo	Medications/ Time, Dosage

Daily Log

Wake up at:

Activity level:

Food and treats

Time	Food and Amount

Water Intake

Time	Amount

Bathroom/Pee, Poo	Medications/ Time, Dosage

Daily Log

Wake up at:

Activity level:

Food and treats

Time	Food and Amount

Water Intake

Time	Amount

Bathroom/Pee, Poo	Medications/ Time, Dosage

Daily Log

Wake up at:

Activity level:

Food and treats

Time	Food and Amount

Water Intake

Time	Amount

Bathroom/Pee, Poo	Medications/ Time, Dosage

Daily Log

Wake up at:

Activity level:

Food and treats

Time	Food and Amount

Water Intake

Time	Amount

Bathroom/Pee, Poo	Medications/ Time, Dosage

Daily Log

Wake up at:

Activity level:

Food and treats

Time	Food and Amount

Water Intake

Time	Amount

Bathroom/Pee, Poo	Medications/ Time, Dosage

Daily Log

Wake up at:

Activity level:

Food and treats

Time	Food and Amount

Water Intake

Time	Amount

Bathroom/Pee, Poo	Medications/ Time, Dosage

Daily Log

Wake up at:

Activity level:

Food and treats

Time	Food and Amount

Water Intake

Time	Amount

Bathroom/Pee, Poo	Medications/ Time, Dosage

Daily Log

Wake up at:

Activity level:

Food and treats

Time	Food and Amount

Water Intake

Time	Amount

Bathroom/Pee, Poo	Medications/ Time, Dosage

Daily Log

Wake up at:

Activity level:

Food and treats

Time	Food and Amount

Water Intake

Time	Amount

Bathroom/Pee, Poo	Medications/ Time, Dosage

Daily Log

Wake up at:

Activity level:

Food and treats

Time	Food and Amount

Water Intake

Time	Amount

Bathroom/Pee, Poo	Medications/ Time, Dosage

Made in the USA
Monee, IL
28 December 2021

87429593R00057